D0554377

HIP-HOP
CULTURE

By Judy Dodge Cummings

CONTENT CONSULTANT
RACHEL RAIMIST, PHD
ASSOCIATE PROFESSOR
DEPARTMENT OF JOURNALISM & CREATIVE MEDIA
UNIVERSITY OF ALABAMA

Essential Library

An Imprint of Abdo Publishing | abdopublishing.com

abdopublishing.com

Published by Abdo Publishing, a division of ABDO, PO Box 398166, Minneapolis, Minnesota 55439. Copyright © 2018 by Abdo Consulting Group, Inc. International copyrights reserved in all countries. No part of this book may be reproduced in any form without written permission from the publisher. Essential Library™ is a trademark and logo of Abdo Publishing.

Printed in the United States of America, North Mankato, Minnesota
042017
092017

 THIS BOOK CONTAINS
RECYCLED MATERIALS

Cover Photo: Shutterstock Images
Interior Photos: iStockphoto, 5, 34, 92–93; Jack Vartoogian/Archive Photos/ Getty Images, 6; Jim Wells/AP Images, 9; Bebeto Matthews/AP Images, 11, 73; David Corio/Michael Ochs Archives/Getty Images, 13; Shutterstock Images, 16, 69, 96–97; Featureflash Photo Agency/Shutterstock Images, 21; Seth Wenig/ AP Images, 23; Daniel DeSlover/Zuma Press/Alamy, 25; Al Pereira/Michael Ochs Archives/Getty, 27, 65; Photos 12/Alamy, 29; Christian Mueller/Shutterstock Images, 33; Richard B. Levine/Newscom, 36; Reuters/Alamy, 40–41; age fotostock/ Alamy, 43; Philippe Gras/Alamy, 45; Linda Vartoogian/Archive Photos/Getty Images, 49; Michael Ochs Archives/Getty Images, 53; Gary Gershoff/Getty Images Entertainment/Getty Images, 56; Time & Life Pictures/The LIFE Picture Collection/ Getty Images, 59; The Advertising Archives/Alamy, 61; LesByerley/iStockphoto, 63; Jamie Lamor Thompson/Shutterstock Images, 66; Julie Markes/AP Images, 74; Shawn Baldwin/AP Images, 76; KPA/Heritage Images/Glow Images, 79; Matt Sayles/Invision/AP Images, 82; Jeff Fusco/Getty Images Entertainment/Getty Images, 85; Derrick Salters/Shutterstock Images, 87; Stephen Chernin/AP Images, 88; Christian Bertrand/Shutterstock Images, 94

Editor: Kari Cornell
Series Designer: Jake Nordby

Publisher's Cataloging-in-Publication Data
Names: Dodge Cummings, Judy, author.
Title: Hip-hop culture / by Judy Dodge Cummings.
Description: Minneapolis, MN : Abdo Publishing, 2018. | Series: Hip-hop insider | Includes bibliographical references and index.
Identifiers: LCCN 2016962247 | ISBN 9781532110276 (lib. bdg.) | ISBN 9781680788129 (ebook)
Subjects: LCSH: Hip-hop--Juvenile literature. | Popular culture--Juvenile literature.
Classification: DDC 306.4--dc23
LC record available at http://lccn.loc.gov/2016962247

CONTENTS

CHAPTER 1
BORN FROM ASHES 4

CHAPTER 2
FROM DJ TO PRODUCER 12

CHAPTER 3
RAPPING MCs 22

CHAPTER 4
TAGGING AND BOMBING 32

CHAPTER 5
ROCKING AND POPPING 42

CHAPTER 6
LOOKING FRESH 52

CHAPTER 7
SPEAKING HIP-HOP 62

CHAPTER 8
STAGE AND SCREEN 72

CHAPTER 9
HIP-HOP ACTIVISM 84

Timeline 98
Essential Facts 100
Glossary 102
Additional Resources 104

Source Notes 106
Index 110
About the Author 112

1 BORN FROM ASHES

The school year was just around the corner, and Cindy Campbell was short of cash to buy new clothes. She and her brother Clive, an aspiring DJ who called himself Kool Herc, decided to have a dance party and charge admission. The date was set for August 11, 1973. The place was the recreation, or rec, room of the Campbell's public housing complex in the South Bronx, a borough of New York City.

The Campbell family had migrated from Jamaica a few years earlier, bringing that island's vibrant musical traditions with. The father, Keith, collected records and was the soundman for a rhythm-and-blues (R&B) band. He had invested in a new sound system but could not figure out

In the spirit of DJ Kool Herc, a DJ spins records on a turntable. DJs often

On August 10, 2013, DJ Kool Herc, *second from right*, his sister Cindy Campbell, *center*, and DJ Coke La Rock, *right*, performed at the Fortieth Anniversary of Hip-Hop Culture in Central Park.

how to maximize its volume. Keith ordered his son not to touch the equipment. But knowing he was a better technician than his dad, Herc began to tinker with the sound system one day when Keith was out.

Soon Herc had the speakers pounding so loudly he did not hear his father return. "Where the noise come from?" Keith Campbell yelled. Herc prepared for a tongue-lashing. Instead his dad said, "Raas claat, man! We 'ave sound!"[1] Father and son compromised. Herc would play records when his dad's band was on intermission, and in turn, he could use the sound system to DJ at parties.

Hip-Hop's Birthday

On August 11, teenagers packed the rec room at 1520 Sedgwick Avenue. Herc played funk and soul music and kept the crowd engaged with jaunty banter. The crowd loved it, and his reputation as a DJ soared.

Herc moved on to deejaying at house parties, block parties, and concerts in nearby Cedar Park. He noticed people got fired up on the dance floor during the instrumental breaks in a song when drum solos were featured. So Herc developed a technique called the merry-go-round to extend these breaks by using two turntables and two copies of the same record. He was altering recorded music to create a new sound. This was the beginning of hip-hop. Most people define hip-hop as a genre of music, but it is bigger than that. Hip-hop is a shared set of values, beliefs, and behaviors—in other words, a culture. This

KOOL HERC ON HIP-HOP

Clive "DJ Kool Herc" Campbell holds a place in the heart of fans as the man who gave birth to hip-hop, but he did not do it alone. "The parties I gave happened to catch on," Herc said. "Then the younger generation came in and . . . [put] their spin on what I had started. I set down the blueprint, and all the architects started adding on this level and that level."[2]

way of life was born in the 1970s in the South Bronx, a community facing many troubles.

"City of Death"

The South Bronx, where Cindy Campbell and Kool Herc grew up, was labeled "America's worst slum" in the 1970s.[3]

SEVEN-MILE TRENCH

In the first half of the 1900s, the Bronx was a stable, diverse community. Following World War II (1939–1945), manufacturing jobs moved to the suburbs. In 1953, urban planners dug a seven-mile (11 km) trench through the Bronx to build an expressway to link the suburbs with downtown Manhattan. A subway line, three railroads, 100 streets, 60,000 homes, and 170,000 people had to be rerouted, removed, or relocated.[5] Neighborhoods were fragmented as single-family homes were demolished and replaced with high-rise, low-income apartments. Middle-class whites and blacks moved out. Poor blacks and Caribbean and Puerto Rican immigrants moved in.

Iron fire escapes crisscrossed high-rise brick tenements. Children climbed over rubble from burned-out buildings on their way home from school. Prostitutes negotiated deals on sidewalks as unemployed men played cards in abandoned cafés. Elderly women passed rusty automobiles, heroin addicts, and burning barrels of trash on their way to the corner bodega for a gallon of milk.

Populated by poor African-American, Caribbean, and Latino families, the South Bronx had lost

600,000 manufacturing jobs in the previous decade. The community's per capita income was half of what people earned in the rest of New York City.[4] Heroin addiction was epidemic, and rival gangs ruled the streets.

"Trying to define hip-hop is a little like asking what air is.**"**[9]

—*former* Los Angeles Times *music critic Ann Powers, now with NPR*

New York's fiscal crisis made matters worse. Thousands of firefighters were laid off, and neighborhood fire stations closed. Between 1973 and 1977, arsonists set more than 12,000 fires each year, destroying 5,000 apartment buildings.[6] On July 13, 1977, a citywide power outage

Abandoned buildings, urban decay, poverty, and crime characterized the Bronx in the 1970s. This devastation gave rise to hip-hop music and culture.

BLACKOUT

DJ Grandmaster Caz was in a park spinning records when the power went out in New York City on July 13, 1977. He saw opportunity and seized it. Caz stole an audio mixer that night and says many others looted sound equipment, too. He believes the blackout accelerated the rise of hip-hop because people who could not afford DJ equipment got it for free when New York City went dark.

shut off the lights in New York City for 36 hours, and looters pillaged businesses.[7] A doctor who ran a clinic in the South Bronx labeled it "a Necropolis—city of death."[8]

But the South Bronx was not dead. The hip-hop dance parties Herc threw were proof of that. Instead, the borough was alive with vibrant and creative people. When there wasn't a party, people gathered on street corners and in parks to listen as poets chanted rhymes or DJs played James Brown songs. Dancers combined martial arts and gymnastics to create daring new moves. Bold, colorful graffiti shouted from the sides of buildings and passing trains. By the end of the 1970s, hip-hop culture would enter mainstream America and change the world.

People born between the years 1965 and 1984 are considered part of the hip-hop generation. But hip-hop does not belong only to them. It is a global culture that young people of today continue to define and transform.

In April 2003, DJ Kool Herc, who is credited as the father of hip-hop, was named one of New York's most influential people.

2 FROM DJ TO PRODUCER

Around six o'clock on an evening in 1975, hundreds of teenagers gather for a party in a public park in the South Bronx, New York City. Graffiti writers have turned dirty brick and concrete into a vibrant backdrop of wild-style-lettered art. A DJ plugs his sound system into a streetlight. He plays records on two turntables, moving the vinyl back and forth to create a scratching sound.

A crowd of African-American and Latino teenagers moves toward the music. While the beat rocks, the masters of ceremonies (known as MCs or emcees) try to out-rhyme each other in rapid-fire improv. The best dancers form a cypher, the circular space in which these kids,

DJ Grandmaster Flash mixes it up at the turntable in the early 1980s.

called b-boys and b-girls, take turns flipping, freezing, and spinning. Everyone from dancer, to DJ, to writer and rapper is intensely focused on showcasing his or her individuality.

Four elements formed the foundation of hip-hop culture in the early 1970s: deejaying, emceeing, break dancing, and graffiti writing. While no element was more artistic or valuable than another, it was the DJs who created the musical sound that allowed hip-hop to break out of the Bronx.

DJ Innovations

The job of a disc jockey is to entertain by playing prerecorded music that inspires people to dance. In the early 1970s, some DJ pioneers from New York City began turning records and turntables into musical instruments, manipulating them to create totally new sounds. These men and women developed oversized personalities and launched the soundtrack of hip-hop culture.

The invention of the breakbeat was the first step in DJs becoming music

> "After I did it for the first time, there was no turnin' back—everybody was coming to the party for that particular part of my set."[1]
>
> —DJ Kool Herc on the merry-go-round technique

makers. This was DJ Kool Herc's invention. He noticed dancers became most excited during the instrumental breaks in a song. So he chose records based on the beat in their breaks. Then he developed a technique called the merry-go-round. Using two copies of the same vinyl record on two turntables, Herc played the break in one song. Then a split second before the break ended, he would pivot to the second turntable and play the break on that record. Back and forth Herc spun, turning a 15-second break into five minutes or more.

Joseph Saddler, better known as Grandmaster Flash, liked the merry-go-round but found it difficult to drop the needle precisely where the break began. So he invented the quick-mix theory. Flash marked up his records, sectioning off each break like a clock. Then he plugged his turntables into a piece of equipment called a mixer and donned a headset so he could hear each album separately. When the second record was cued up to the break, Flash cranked up the volume on that turntable and lowered it on the other one. The beat played seamlessly from one record to the next.

In 1975, a teenage DJ named Theodore Livingston (Grand Wizard Theodore) accidentally discovered a technique called scratching. He was in his room one day

Doug E. Fresh popularized beatboxing, in which a human produces sounds such as drumbeats or record scratches.

playing records when his mom entered, yelling at him to turn down the music. Startled, Livingstone pressed his fingers on the record to stop it. The album kept rocking and made a scratching sound. Soon after his discovery, scratching made its way to local clubs. Today scratching is a staple of hip-hop music.

Beat juggling fundamentally changed the role of the DJ. In this technique, a DJ plays two records at the same time, usually the same song, but he or she manipulates the records to create a new sound. The DJ is not just alternating between two records like Herc and Flash did to extend the break. With beat juggling, the DJ is actually reconfiguring the song. So he or she might play an extra snare solo or a key vocal phrase on one record while a song plays on the second record. Or the DJ might scratch one record while playing the break on the second one. As technology improved, beat juggling set the stage for DJs to transition from performing live to producing music in a studio.

By the 1990s, these DJ techniques became their own musical genre called turntablism. Turntablists

BEATBOXING

Not all beats come from records. Beatboxers are artists who use their bodies as instruments. With their mouths, tongues, and throats, they create the sounds of bass or snare drums or even the scratching on a record. Doug E. Fresh, known as the first human beatbox, is credited with introducing the hip-hop community to beatboxing. Fresh's flawless drum-machine imitations were first recorded on the song "Pass the Budda" with Spoonie Gee and DJ Spivey in 1983. But he gained fame in hip-hop circles in 1984 when he performed in the movie *Beat Street* with the pioneering hip-hop group Treacherous Three. Since then, Doug E. Fresh has been the beatboxer by which all others are judged. In recent years, Antoinette "Butterscotch" Clinton has gained fame as a female beatboxer. She composes original music, plays several instruments, and can even beatbox while playing the piano.

do not just play records. They make original music by manipulating records to create different accents, sounds, and rhythms.

Zulu Nation

It was a gang leader turned DJ who developed the first hip-hop organization and the philosophical framework that formed the foundation of the culture. Afrika Bambaataa, a member of the Black Spades gang, took advantage of a 1971 truce between rival gangs to turn his life in a new direction. He became a DJ. Bambaataa's playlist was diverse—funk, soul, rock, salsa, even clips of political speeches, and more.

After the death of his cousin from street violence and an eye-opening trip to Africa, Bambaataa decided to use music to improve his community. He founded the Universal Zulu Nation in 1975 and brought DJs, dancers, graffiti writers, and MCs together at the Bronx

MERCEDES LADIES

The Mercedes Ladies, formed in 1976, was the first all-female hip-hop crew. The group had four MCs, two or three DJs, and 14 or 15 supporting members. They shared the stage with some of the most important men of early hip-hop, including Kool Herc, Afrika Bambaataa, and Grandmaster Flash. Sheri Sher, the founder of the group, said these men were extremely supportive and acted like brothers. However, she added, "Because we was all females, . . . we had to make our reputation stand when we went out there."[2]

River Community Center. The Zulu Nation's motto was Peace, Love, Unity and Having Fun. Bambaataa developed a moral code he called the Seven Infinity Lessons. These lessons drew from both Christianity and Islam and celebrated African heritage. Zulu Nation chapters sprung up throughout New York and neighboring states.

When the media asked Bambaataa about the music, he called it "hip" because it was hip or trendy, and "hop" because when you heard it, you couldn't help but dance to it. Eventually the phrase came to represent the culture developing around him. From then on, this urban youth culture was referred to as hip-hop.

Beat Makers

By 1979, it appeared the DJ was going the way of the dinosaur. That year the Sugarhill Gang recorded the first hip-hop song—"Rapper's Delight." Other recordings quickly followed. Rappers took center stage as live bands or drum machines made the music, not DJs.

Then DJ Marley Marl discovered a new way of using a digital sampling. Samplers were equipped with programmed sounds from the violin, piano, and other instruments. But Marl used the machine to sample a section of another artist's record. Sampling involves taking

MIXTAPES

Mixtapes help artists break into the music industry. Aspiring stars sample songs from other artists and blend them into a new interpretation. They compile a collection of these creations on a cassette tape or CD, the mixtape. Artists who are not represented by a record label can distribute their mixtapes cheaply to build a fan base. The rapper 50 Cent gained a huge following from giving away his mixtapes. As a result, a major record label signed him, and he became a hip-hop superstar. Nicki Minaj, a rapper from Queens, New York City, also rose to fame after releasing three mixtapes between 2007 and 2009. In 2010, Minaj made history when she became the first female solo artist to have seven singles on the *Billboard* charts at the same time.

snippets of recorded songs and mixing them together to create something new. For example, if a DJ wanted a saxophone sound but did not want to hire a live musician, he could lift sax sections from different albums, cut them to the length he wanted, change the pitch or even stretch the sound, and put them in a certain order.

DJs had been doing live sampling when they did beat juggling in clubs. But as technology improved, they could record their own musical interpretations in studios and compile songs on mixtapes to share with fans. DJs became music producers.

Sampling became the blueprint for hip-hop music by the 1980s. However, the practice was controversial. Some producers used samples without getting permission from

Nicki Minaj, who rose to fame as a result of her mixtapes, poses for a photo at the signing for her album *Pink Friday: Roman Reloaded* in 2012.

the original artists. Many people considered this a theft of intellectual property. Lawsuits eventually established that producers had to get permission and pay for original samples they used.

3 RAPPING MCs

In the summer of 1975, DJ Grandmaster Flash had perfected his technique of mixing a track and thought he had the perfect blend of beat, rhythm, and melody. Excited, he played the song for an audience. The crowd did not dance or smile. They just stared at him. "I cried for like a week," Flash recalled.[1]

When his tears dried, Flash realized it took more than technical precision to rock a room. He needed someone to excite the crowd. Flash turned to his friend Robert Keith "Cowboy" Wiggins. Cowboy worked the crowd for Flash with a call-and-response routine. "Say ho!" Cowboy would yell, and the crowd would holler back, "Ho!" He ordered dancers to "Throw your

Flash, *center*, and Cowboy, *right*, formed Grandmaster Flash and the Furious Five, which entered the Rock and Roll Hall of Fame in 2007.

hands in the air and wave 'em like you just don't care," and they did.[2] Cowboy and other crowd-pleasing showmen were the first MCs. Emceeing is the oral element of hip-hop culture, what today is more commonly known as rap.

MCs started out as DJ helpers. The initials MC meant different things depending on the task. One minute an MC would be the "microphone controller," and the next he or she needed to "move the crowd" or maybe do a "mic check." The MC's main job was to excite and control the crowd.

While a DJ needed a good beat, MCs needed outsized personalities. The first MCs set the style. At Herc's parties, Coke La Rock would call out, "There's no story can't be told, there's no horse can't be rode."[3] Cowboy hooked up with Melle Mel and Kidd Creole. The trio composed witty rhymes, playing off each other as they revved up the room. Many of their lines were spontaneous, but they also rewrote lyrics from soul or R&B songs or from the Last Poets, a group of politically charged spoken-word poets from the civil rights movement of the 1960s.

"Rap is something you do, hip-hop is something you live."

—KRS-One in "Hip-Hop Vs. Rap"[4]

Melle Mel, a.k.a. Melvin Glover, rose to fame as a member of the Furious Five.

Birth of Battle Rap

MCs grew more sophisticated over time as they competed to see who could come up with the best razor-sharp, witty lyrics. Soon the crowd came for the rapping as much as for the DJ's mixes. This was the beginning of battle rap. The first and most famous standoff took place in December 1982 at the Harlem World club when Kool Moe Dee of the Treacherous Three challenged rapper Busy Bee Starski. Busy Bee, who had just bragged in rap about being the best MC, left the room, assuming no one would challenge him. Then Kool Moe Dee took the mic, and the rest is history. Kool Moe Dee dissed Busy Bee's rap, word for

THE DOZENS

Verbal sparring has long roots in African-American communities. "Playing the dozens" is a contest between two people, usually young black men or teens, in which they try to out-insult each other. Often the quips are done in rhyme. Yo mama jokes are a modern form of the dozens that have become popular among teenagers in general. The dozens is deeply rooted in US history, possibly dating back to the era of slavery. Word battles are central to an MC's art.

word. With his response, Kool Moe Dee had launched an entirely new style of rap.

Transformation

As battle rap transformed the genre, hip-hop music entered a golden age, which ran from the mid-1980s to the early 1990s. MCs with diverse styles and a variety of messages hit the big time. Run-D.M.C. was a breakout success, becoming the first hip-hop group with a gold album in 1984. LL Cool J had sex appeal that sold on an international level. The Beastie Boys proved that white boys could rap. Public Enemy broadcast a political message that some found abrasive and others inspiring. Salt-N-Pepa and Queen Latifah demonstrated the power of the female MC.

In the early 1990s, a new generation of MCs emerged in South Central Los Angeles. The new MCs' sound and style began dominating hip-hop music. MCs rapped in first person about being hustlers, gang members, and cop

The members of Salt-N-Pepa, made up of Cheryl James (Salt), Sandra Denton (Pepa) and Deidra Roper (DJ Spinderella), strike a pose outside of Bayside Studios in Queens in 1989.

RAP GOES MAINSTREAM

In 1979, Sylvia Robinson formed the Sugarhill Gang and recorded the first rap single. "Rapper's Delight" was easy to dance to with lighthearted lyrics, and it was performed without a DJ. Although some in the hip-hop community didn't consider the song true to hip-hop's roots, the song jumped to the American Top 40 and then went international. Artists and record companies scrambled to make deals. The music of hip-hop culture was about to become big business, with MCs front and center.

killers. Someone coined the term *gangsta rap*, and the label stuck.

In 1988, the group Niggaz With Attitude, or N.W.A, released its debut album, *Straight Outta Compton*. It quickly sold 750,000 copies.[5] The music not only appealed to inner-city black youth for portraying their lives so realistically, but its anger and alienation also resonated with suburban, middle-class white kids eager to rebel. However, while rap fans loved the album, many others did not. The track titled "F*** Tha Police" was condemned by President George H. W. Bush, and the Federal Bureau of Investigation (FBI) accused the group of inciting violence against police officers. But the album went gold in only six weeks. N.W.A's notoriety and financial success started a trend.

Soon gangsta rap was being played on pop radio. The success of this subgenre turned some former gang

Ice Cube and Dr. Dre, *top left and right*, members of N.W.A, are photographed with cast members from the film *Straight Outta Compton* in 2015.

members into MC millionaires, but it also led to controversy and censorship.

Battle for Control

By the mid-1990s, the line between rapping about the gangster life and living the gangster life grew blurry. A rivalry developed between two competing record labels—West Coast–based Death Row Records and New York City's Bad Boy Entertainment. Suge Knight, who headed Death Row Records, was believed to be a former

BREEDING GROUND FOR GANGSTA RAP

In the 1980s, 131 manufacturing plants shut their doors in South Central Los Angeles, and 124,000 people lost their jobs. California taxpayers capped property taxes, and with no revenue, the public education system deteriorated. In 1983, the unemployment rate for teenagers in South Central Los Angeles was 50 percent, and the poverty rate was more than 30 percent.[6] Crime became a way to survive, and those survival stories infused rap lyrics.

Bloods gang member. He shaped the careers of many MCs, including Dr. Dre, Snoop Dogg, and Tupac Shakur. Bad Boy Entertainment, headed up by Sean "Puff Daddy" Combs, helped Craig Mack and the Notorious B.I.G. (Biggie) become stars. MCs from each company aimed verbal arrows at each other in rap lyrics. Then, in September 1996, someone gunned down Tupac Shakur in Las Vegas, killing him. At a party in March 1997, Biggie was shot and killed in Los Angeles. Both cases remain a mystery.

While gangsta rap did not disappear, the murders of Tupac and Biggie marked a turning point. Some rappers wound up in jail, and others began making a different type of music. As the world entered a new millennium, voices in the African-American community spoke out against the offensive language in gangsta rap. The tastes of hip-hop fans also changed. A study conducted by

Music Television (MTV) found young people wanted more emotional connection to their music. When gangsta rap began, its raw emotional core had appealed to listeners. A decade later, they found the music heartless.

Some artists agreed. In 2006, the rapper Nas released the album *Hip Hop Is Dead*. He believed hip-hop culture was in a vulnerable place, and if the music could not evolve, the culture was going to die out. University of Pennsylvania Afro-American and religious studies professor Michael Dyson found the fact that MCs were criticizing the state of their art to be a hopeful sign. It meant hip-hop culture was still alive. "Horrible hip-hop must die so regal hip-hop can live," Dyson said. "Hip-hop is dead. Long live hip-hop."[7] Through experimentation and reflection, MCs continue to evolve and make lyrics that remain relevant for modern youth.

PROPHET FOR THE FUTURE

Since Tupac Shakur's death in 1996, associates have released eight albums of previously unpublished material. His music often outsells that of living MCs. A 2004 Harvard conference explored why the artist remains immortal. One reason is Tupac's lyrics explore timeless themes such as life and death and judgment versus forgiveness. Also, the artist devoured literature from many genres as he wrote his lyrics. To understand his words, Tupac's fans must read and think deeply. Professor Michael Dyson characterized Tupac as "a thinking man's verbal outlaw."[8]

4 TAGGING AND BOMBING

In the late 1960s, a boy named Demetrius lived on W. 183rd Street in New York City's Uptown neighborhood. One day he saw the signature, called a tag, another kid had scrawled across a wall—JULIO 124. Demetrius decided to try tagging too. He adopted the code name TAKI 183 and tagged buildings from Uptown to Manhattan and the subway cars in between. Other teens noticed, and graffiti art exploded in New York City.

Motivation

Graffiti is writing or drawing on a public structure without permission. The practice has been around for centuries, but the graffiti of hip-hop culture emerged in the mid-1960s,

Colorful graffiti tags even mark the rooftops in New York City.

Hundreds of taggers have laid claim to the walls in this view of the Manhattan skyline.

first in Philadelphia, Pennsylvania, and then New York City. Graffiti writers left signatures, messages, and art everywhere with high visibility. The act of creating graffiti was illegal and that added to its appeal.

Graffiti writing was popular before hip-hop music and dance. It is considered one of the elements of hip-hop culture because the graffiti writers' rebelliousness, individuality, and desire for fame was echoed by the DJs, MCs, and b-boys/b-girls who emerged a few years later. Although graffiti is considered part of hip-hop culture, not all graffiti artists identified with hip-hop. Author Jeff Chang called graffiti writers "The advance guard of a new culture."[1]

The reasons for writing graffiti varied from artist to artist. TAKI 183 admitted that he was "just killing time."[2] MICO said that all writers had one thing in common: "We wanted to be famous."[3] LSD OM believed rage drove many writers. He said, "People were . . . upset that they didn't have a voice in the world. . . . Writing was a way of

> "Graffiti is a term that the *New York Times* coined, and it denigrates the art because it was invented by youth of color. Had it been invented by the children of the rich or the influential, it would have been branded avant-garde Pop Art."[4]
>
> —*Graffiti writer MICO*

Graffiti artist Lady Pink works on the side of a train in Chelsea, Manhattan, on August 24, 2005, at the first ever Graffiti Block Party.

saying, 'Don't make a decision without consulting us.'"[5] Artist Lady Pink said graffiti was "a way of defining what our generation is like. We defend our territory, whatever space we steal to paint on, we defend it fiercely."[6] The tag name of a writer was a brand of sorts. The more frequently a tag appeared around the city, and the higher the quality of the writing, the more street cred, or credibility, the artist earned.

> "The world could take a great lesson in conquering racism by giving everybody a can of spray paint!"[7]
>
> —Graffiti writer LIL SOUL 159

Contagious Art

The quantity of tags and styles of writing evolved. TOPCAT 126 moved from Philadelphia to New York, bringing with him Broadway

Elegant writing, a slim, tall style of letters. Tools changed too. First, writers used felt pens and Magic Markers, but spray paint soon became the medium of choice.

Writers developed their own communities. The park bench at 149th Street in the Bronx was called the Writer's Bench. Teens gathered there to compare work, share techniques, and get each other's autographs. Other city neighborhoods had similar hangouts for writers.

Because most DJs, dancers, and rappers were black and Latino, people assumed the graffiti writers of hip-hop culture were too. T-KID 170 said, "The truth of the matter is that graffiti was multiracial. Black, Hispanic, white—you didn't care, and the guys who did it came in all colors."[8] LIL SOUL 159 agreed. He said, "Any writer will tell you that graffiti tore down the racial barriers of the late 1960s and early 1970s—eradicated them! . . . Once we smelled ink, we were just writers."[9]

CITY STRIKES BACK

In the late 1980s, New York City's transit authority decided to eradicate all graffiti. The city replaced its fleet of trains, secured train yards with razor wire, and put more police on the streets. As soon as graffiti appeared, authorities chemically removed it. One city official declared, "Nothing you do in this [train] yard is gonna see the light of day."[10] Graffiti writing began to decline. No one wanted to create a masterpiece that would immediately be destroyed.

The golden age of New York City's graffiti art was the 1970s. After CHARMIN 65 tagged the Statue of Liberty in 1972, the mayor created a graffiti task force, and it became illegal to carry spray cans into a public building. However, writers outwitted the police and transit authorities trying to apprehend them. The 1974 movie *Death Wish* featured some graffiti writers who became celebrities, which encouraged more youth to pick up paint. Graffiti art covered the city, with some artists going through 50 cans of paint in one night.

TAGBANGING

In the late 1980s, the gang violence in Los Angeles spawned a fad called tagbanging. Young teenagers would mob a city bus, tag it, and rough up the riders. These kids were not true graffiti writers. They were trying to claim territory. The real gangs of LA resented tagbangers, because the kids acted like a gang but did not pay taxes to the Mexican Mafia as other gangs did. Meanwhile, real graffiti writers struggled as they dealt with angry gangs that thought they were tagbangers and media that labeled them thugs. Finally, gang leaders gave the tagbangers an ultimatum—either quit their activity or form real gangs and pay taxes. The tagbanging fad stopped.

Wild Style Goes Global

Film and literature helped spread hip-hop graffiti across the United States in the mid-1980s. The film *Wild Style* was released in 1983, and the book *Subway Art* was published in 1984. Copies of both were passed from friend to friend. Ideas for graffiti art also spread as teens relocated or visited relatives in distant cities.

Print and digital media spread graffiti globally in the mid-1990s. Hip-hop magazine *The Source* featured a graffiti page in each issue. The Internet broke down barriers. *Art Crimes*, the first graffiti website, went online in 1994. Despite the fact that graffiti writing remains a crime almost everywhere, it has gone global, even occurring in nations with restrictive governments.

WHAT'S IN A NAME?

Writers' tag names come from a variety of sources. Some artists simply adapt their own name. So Frank Del Toro became FDT 56. Some writers, such as SUPER STRUT, want to foster a certain image. The writer's past could suggest a name. One man broke his leg and took the name DEAD LEG. The nature of art also generated ideas. At the end of the night, a lot of soap was required to wash the spray paint off one's hands. One graffiti writer called himself LAVA after the brand of soap he used.

The public perception of graffiti in the United States has softened a little since the 1970s. Some graffiti-filled neighborhoods like New York City's Lower East Side are considered hot property. However, these communities are the exception, not the norm. In 2013, an 18-year-old man in Miami was tased by police when they caught him writing on an abandoned building. The man died as a result. In the United States, and most of the world, graffiti remains outlaw art.

GRAFFITI FOR A
GREATER GOOD

In the West African country of Senegal, graffiti writing is legal. The acceptance with which Senegalese society views graffiti has led that country's hip-hop art to develop differently than it has elsewhere.

In the United States, individuals tag walls and subways because the act is forbidden, and artists want to show off their bravery and their bold, unique style. The more magnificent the masterpiece and the greater the chance of detection, the more fame the graffiti writer gets in his community.

Senegal is a poor country with a crumbling infrastructure. Graffiti writing is encouraged by authorities and the public. Writers do not seek individual fame, but instead work together out of a sense of duty. Artists paint walls to beautify neighborhoods and communicate positive messages to fellow citizens.

In the city of Dakar, anyone can openly write graffiti on a public wall in the middle of the day. Some private citizens even "give" walls on their own property to talented artists. Veteran writer Docta says that graffiti writers around the world call Senegal "the paradise of graffiti."[11] The police do not jail a youth they see writing graffiti. Instead, they compliment him or her on the beauty of the art.

Diablos, a graffiti artist who is part of the group Radical Bomb Squad, paints a mural along a highway wall in Dakar, Senegal.

5 ROCKING AND POPPING

When DJ Kool Herc figured out how to extend the instrumental break of a song, he gave the young dancers at his parties what they craved—waves of drum solos that pushed them into a frenzy of movement. Dancers longed for a chance to showcase their unique talents as the DJs did through music, the MCs through lyrics, and the graffiti writers through tagging. Herc called these dancers his break boys, which was shortened to b-boys and b-girls. Hip-hop dance was collectively labeled break dancing or breaking by the media. The term encompasses a wide variety of styles invented by dancers on the streets and in the clubs as they grooved to the music that surrounded them.

A b-boy hits the floor while his friends keep the beat at a New York subway stop in 2010.

The Cypher and Apache Line

Battles between New York City's rival gangs began to cool down in 1971, but on the dance floor, warfare heated up. Each neighborhood had a dance crew, and its goal was to be the best. DJ Jazzy Jay said the attitude of the dancers was, "Okay, we all about our music and we love our music but you come in this area wrong and we all about kicking your [butt]."[1] Competition fueled the whole movement.

GODFATHER OF SOUL

The dance moves of James Brown have significantly influenced hip-hop dance. The legendary soul and rock singer had a career that spanned six decades. Although Brown's career peaked in the 1960s, DJs in the South Bronx were still playing his records in the 1970s, and Brown still performed on television. Young dancers imitated the Godfather of Soul's fancy footwork. DJ Jazzy Jay, who started his career as a b-boy, said, "You could be dancing with your girl and spin away from her, hit the ground, come back up. It was all about 'smooth.'"[2] That smooth was pure James Brown.

B-boys and b-girls developed performance personalities. The Amazing Bobo, Sau Sau, and Charlie Rock were some of the guys in Herc's crew of dancers, called the Herculords. Afrika Bambaataa formed all-male and all-female dance crews, the Zulu King dancers and the Shaka Kings and Queens.

The early b-boys had no choreographed routines. Everything was freestyle. Dancers performed within a

James Brown brought innovation to pop and soul music and also created funk.

cypher, or circular dance space, one at a time. They used any place they could find—someone's basement, a street corner, or a vacant lot. Spectators gathered around the outside of the circle to watch. Once a move caught on, dancers performed its basic structure and then added their own flair. This was how hip-hop dance evolved into ever more athletic and flamboyant styles.

Dance moves were named for what they looked like. The boyoing involved a guy wearing a pom-pom hat. He stretched and wiggled and shook until the ball went "boyoing." In the cork-and-screw, dancers spun down, popped up, and did the splits. In the top rock, dancers remained upright but moved their feet.

Brooklyn uprocking was an aggressive form of dance. Instead of forming a cypher, dancers faced off in a so-called Apache line, a term taken from the gangs' playbook. New gang recruits had to fight their way across a line of gang members armed with fists, chains, and baseball bats. In Brooklyn uprocking, two crews of dancers stood in line facing each other and danced simultaneously. Their jerks and kicks mimicked battle.

Locking and Popping

While breaking gained popularity on the East Coast, funk dance styles took hold on the West Coast. Don Campbell began locking while learning a new dance move. When friends tried to teach him how to do a popular dance called the funky chicken, Campbell kept locking up his shoulder joints and tightening his hands, making a freezing motion. A friend thought the move looked cool and encouraged Campbell to enter some contests. He did and he won. From there he went on to found a dance crew called the Lockers.

Other signature moves were developed by West Coast pioneers. In the

> "We used to b-boy right in the middle of the park with broken glass everywhere. . . . You'd just wipe the glass off your elbows and go right back in."[3]
>
> —DJ Jazzy Jay

boogaloo, every body part moves in a different direction. Key muscles contract when a dancer is popping, making jerky movements. These moves led to adaptations like the strut, the dime, and the slide.

Diverse Dancers

African Americans began breaking, but by the late 1970s its popularity among black teens declined. Then Puerto Rican Americans joined the cyphers. Initially, there was tension between Puerto Ricans and blacks, a kind of cultural turf war as teens wondered if breaking should be just an African-American thing. But the Puerto Ricans kept dancing and introduced new styles that excited everyone.

Puerto Rican dancers focused on floor work. B-boy Richard "Crazy Legs" Colón said the dancing changed because the kids wanted a challenge. "You strive to take

LEARNING TO COUNT

Before she joined the Lockers dance crew, Toni Basil had been trained in ballet. When she tried to teach the crew members how to dance to an eight-step count, they were incredulous. "How do you count soul?" one asked. The group told Basil they had never learned to count beats. The cues they used to know when to move came from the body, not the brain. Adolfo "Shabba-Doo" Quiñones said, "Boom, pop, do boom, pada da boom . . . it's a feeling, you know?"[4]

NOT JUST A MAN'S WORLD

For most of hip-hop's history, women have been absent from leadership roles in the dance industry. They did not perform in big shows, and they were not dance teachers. Michele Byrd-McPhee has been trying to change that. In 2004, she founded the Ladies of Hip-Hop Festival. Women run the entire festival. They dance, judge, emcee, advertise, and raise funds. McPhee recognizes that hip-hop dance has a competitive spirit, but "to have women working together to do something for each other . . . we don't do that enough."[7]

your move to the next level. It's about shock value . . . but keeping it flavor and stylized and making it yours."[5] Spy of the Crazy Commanders was known as "the man of a thousand moves."[6] Propped up by only one hand, his legs and feet flew. Zulu King Robbie Rob wowed crowds with the chair freeze, balancing upside down on one elbow and one toe while his body twisted in the opposite direction.

Women joined crews too, but they had to fight to claim a place in the cypher. Ana "Rockafella" Garcia recalled how one male dancer tried to press against her in a sexual manner. Garcia danced her way out of a tricky situation by straddling the guy's waist, doing a back walkover and sliding between his legs. Then she made fun of him by slapping his butt and pushing him out of the circle. Only one all-female crew was created during this time,

The Rock Steady Crew performs at the Booker T. Washington Junior High School playground in New York City in 1983.

the Dynamic Dolls. One of its dancers, Kim "Kim-a-Kazi" Valente, toured with Run-D.M.C.

Media Exposure Leads to Transformation

The entertainment industry introduced hip-hop dance to the rest of the world. *Wild Style*, released in 1983, was the first film to showcase hip-hop dance. That same year, the romantic drama *Flashdanc*e featured the Rock Steady Crew. The film's unexpected success led to a wave of teen movies featuring hip-hop dancers.

BODY DOUBLE

The climactic scene in the movie *Flashdance* features such complicated dancing that actress Jennifer Beals's female body doubles could not perform it. The director turned to 16-year-old Richard "Crazy Legs" Colón. The teen put on a wig, shaved his mustache, and squeezed into a leotard to do the scene.

Television shows also spread breaking. *Soul Train* began in the 1970s and ran for 36 years, featuring a freestyle dance crew called the Soul Train Gang. The program *Solid Gold* also featured the Solid Gold Dancers, who performed choreographed hip-hop routines. Popular hip-hop dance shows in the 1990s were *The Grind* and *The Party Machine*.

Media attention changed hip-hop dance. Power moves such as head spinning became the dominant style by the 1980s because they wowed audiences. In reality, these moves were not as challenging as the original dance forms, because physics propelled dancers through spins.

To satisfy consumer demand, dance studios around the world now feature hip-hop lessons. However, the teachers are often people with no understanding of the broader hip-hop culture. Commercial hip-hop dance simply copies moves seen on rap videos. Hip-hop dance teacher Emilio "Buddha Stretch" Austin said, "A lot of teachers are . . . just teaching the steps . . . They don't know the culture. If all you see is Britney Spears, you think that's hip-hop, but that's never been hip-hop."[8] This kind of pseudo-hip-hop dance violates the culture's principle to keep it real.

Preservation

Competition has been at the heart of hip-hop dance since it began, and competitions keep the dance vibrant today. Freestyle Session was founded in 1997 in California and has since become part of the Pro Breaking Tour, where dancers may compete in events hosted around the world. Hip Hop International began in 2002 and runs live and televised dance competitions. Battle of the Year, with qualifying events held around the globe, is believed to be the biggest stand-alone competition. Street Dance Kemp holds a convention and competition every summer during which male and female dancers compete in crews or solo. The United Kingdom, Japan, and Australia also hold educational and competitive hip-hop dance events each year. Dancers from Samoa to Vietnam to South Africa and beyond come to groove. B-boys might not be on every street corner of the inner cities, but hip-hop dance has reached every corner of the globe.

you got roaches and 10 people living in an apartment, the only way you can . . . feel some kind of status is what you have on your body."[2]

When hip-hop culture was born, fashion was connected to both neighborhood and art. Kids from Brooklyn wore Clarks brand shoes and Kangol brand hats. Brooklyn had a high population of Jamaican immigrants who brought these styles to the United States. The baggy hoody was first worn by graffiti artists to hide spray cans in their pockets and their faces in hoods. The b-boys and b-girls popularized certain shoe brands such as Fila, PUMA, and Nike.

Sneakers Are Hip

When the hip-hop group Run-D.M.C. released a gold record in 1984, the group's style took the spotlight alongside their music. The trio wore gold chains, track suits, Kangols or fedoras, and Adidas Superstar sneakers with no laces and the tongues hanging out. The group's 1986 single "My Adidas" set a look that swept the nation and connected hip-hop fashion to the corporate world.

On the surface, "My Adidas" was a love song to a tennis shoe, but it had deeper meaning for the band. Darryl "DMC" McDaniels felt society viewed urban black youth as problems. The song was a way to let the world know the hip-hop generation had aspirations and was intelligent.

During Run-D.M.C.'s 1986 tour, a senior employee of Adidas attended the group's concert in Madison Square Garden. He was stunned at the sight of thousands of fans lifting Adidas shoes over their heads as the trio rapped the shoe song. Within the week, Run-D.M.C. had a million-dollar endorsement deal with the company. Band members were featured in Adidas ads, and the sale of the company's products soared. The very urban look of this rap group spread across the United States, from suburbs to small towns.

COMPANIES FIGHT THE TREND

Regardless of the money to be made, some companies had no intentions of trying to lure hip-hop youth to their brands. A Carhartt executive said it was great that urban teens liked to wear his company's workwear clothes, "But we will never go after that market aggressively."[3] The former fashion editor of hip-hop magazine the *Source* believed these companies were afraid that if their clothing line was popular in the urban black community, it would "cheapen their brand."[4]

Branding Hip-Hop

In the early 1990s, hip-hop clothes were big and baggy, for female rappers as well as male. Tall or short, fat or thin, many rappers favored XXXL t-shirts, baggy jeans,

Rapper A$AP Rocky wears a Tommy Hilfiger sweater while on stage for his "Under the Influence of Music" tour in August 2013.

and Timberland boots. As the decade progressed, which side of the country artists came from altered their looks. New York rappers wore Carhartt pants and bubble vests, while those from the West Coast preferred flannel shirts buttoned all the way up and Chuck Taylor athletic shoes. Fans who wanted to imitate this look could afford to because these brands were inexpensive.

Then some hip-hop celebrities turned to higher-end designers, including Nautica, Polo Ralph Lauren, and Gucci. This was both an aspirational and rebellious fashion statement. These companies did not market to minorities. They advertised to white, upper-class customers, and clothing prices were steep. Buying these preppy brands was a way for lower-class, urban kids of color to temporarily escape the poverty of their environment while at the same time thumbing their noses at companies that ignored them.

Hip-hoppers wore these brands differently than the rich whites who traditionally purchased them. Billy Ceisler, an executive of the marketing company SRC, believed hip-hop youth were sending a message to American elites that said, "I can wear what you wear. I'm gonna rock it differently—I'm gonna wear my hat to the side and everything big and baggy . . . you're no better than me."[5] Then a designer came along who embraced the hip-hop generation rather than excluding it.

Tommy Hilfiger wanted to design clothes that were "preppy and cool."[6] He did not set out to dress rap stars, but by the early 1990s, his brand was synonymous with hip-hop cool. Hilfiger came up with the low-riding jeans and underwear band look. According to fashion critic Coltrane Curtis, Hilfiger took this design from "street corner culture" where men would be at work with a hammer in their pockets weighing down their jeans.[7]

In 1992, when rapper Grand Puba gave a shout-out in the song "What's the 411?," calling "Tommy Hilfiger top gear," Hilfiger invited Puba to stop by his showroom. Puba

ALWAYS ON THE JOB

As a hip-hop clothing designer, Marc Ecko was always looking out for trends. Once he was eating lunch in a New Jersey mall when he spotted a kid in an olive jacket with hundreds of straight pins sticking up from his collar. Ecko asked the teen why he did that to his jacket. The boy replied, "So no one can grab me from behind."[9] Ecko put the boy in his next fashion show.

and his band walked out with $20,000 in free clothes.[8] The musicians wore these outfits for video shoots and performances. Before long, Tommy Hilfiger was the hottest brand on the street. This relationship validated hip-hop culture too. When Hilfiger appeared with rappers at events or in ads, it told the nation this culture had clout.

FUBU

In the 1990s, some entrepreneurs decided to create their own lines of street wear. These designers were young and believed they understood hip-hop kids more than the middle-aged, white executives who ran most clothing companies. In 1992, Keith Perrin, Daymond John, Carl Brown, and J. Alexander Martin, all from Queens, founded FUBU. Their mission was to create a fashion line that acknowledged and catered to African-American youth.

When rapper Grand Puba, *right*, mentioned Tommy Hilfiger, *left*, in the song "What's the 411?," sales of the Hilfiger brand skyrocketed among the young hip-hop community.

To get exposure from a well-known rapper, the group camped outside LL Cool J's house. When he emerged, they begged him to pose for a photograph dressed in one of their shirts. LL Cool J was willing to help out some guys from the neighborhood. Within seven years, FUBU was a multimillion-dollar business.

Hip-hop celebrities saw the success of these black-owned companies and wanted a piece of the pie. Stars such as Sean Combs and Jay Z became business moguls and opened restaurants, bought sports teams, and started their own fashion lines.

TIGHT CLOTHES CONTROVERSY

In 2008, the rap group Thug Slaughter Force released the single "No Tight Clothes." It slammed male hip-hop performers for wearing formfitting pants and shirts, jeweled belts, and carrying man bags. Band member Blanco the Don said these rappers dressed and acted like gay men but rapped about the "gangster lifestyle."[10] He said this was hypocritical. The group's YouTube video featured the band striding down the streets of Brooklyn in extra-large T-shirts emblazoned with the words "Tight Clothes" crossed out with a red slash. Critics claimed this song was pure homophobia, something for which rap music has long been criticized.

Fashion for a New Century

As the new century dawned, attitudes changed, and hip-hop fashions followed suit. In 2007, Kanye West appeared in a video for his single "Stronger" dressed in formfitting jeans and a snug T-shirt. Some members of the culture considered this style too feminine, even a sign of homosexuality, but West did not let this criticism change his style. In 2005, he had publicly apologized for past homophobic statements and asked fellow rappers to be more tolerant of gays and lesbians. Both the apology and the clothing from a big-name rapper signaled a change in hip-hop culture.

The blueprint for the hip-hop business empires of Sean Combs and Jay Z has been adopted by younger artists including Pharrell Williams and Kanye West. Luxury labels are emphasized more than sportswear or workwear. Today an artist's clothing represents sophisticated culture and tastes.

However, social critics argue these superstars have abandoned the culture they claim to represent. Bakari Kitwana, author of *The Hip Hop Generation*, questioned whether hip-hop culture had "betrayed its ghetto origins as a voice for the voiceless."[11] The truth is that hip-hop is no longer a culture of the American ghetto. It is a global culture of people both rich and poor, black and white.

Pharrell Williams models for a Chanel advertisement that appeared in British magazines in the 2010s. In 2014, he launched his own clothing line, I Am Other, from fashion brand UNIQLO.

7 SPEAKING HIP-HOP

One of the most defining aspects of any culture is language. Values, beliefs, and history are communicated through spoken and written words and symbols. People who identify with hip-hop culture may speak English, French, Swahili, or Japanese, but they are able to converse in a common tongue that linguists call the Hip-Hop Nation Language (HHNL). There is no country with the name of Hip-Hop on any map. The term "Hip-Hop Nation" refers to the collection of communities around the world that practice hip-hop culture. Members of the Hip-Hop Nation speak a language of slang and rhyme that allows them to communicate across borders.

Rappers and MCs are on the cutting edge of hip-hop language. Through new rhymes and raps, they create and reinvent words to fit their verses.

Characteristics of Hip-Hop Language

HHNL is a form of English with sounds, rhythm, and tone that are heavily influenced by the African experience in the Americas. This language encompasses the way words are pronounced, the tone of the voice, the rhythm of the sentences, and even the silences used by a speaker to convey meaning. HHNL also refers to the attitude of both speaker and listener. Historian and music critic Kamau Brathwaite said HHNL is English that sounds like a "howl, or a shout, or a machine-gun or the wind or a wave."[1]

Rappers invented ways to communicate quickly, powerfully, and poetically. Words were clipped. So disrespect became "dis" and neighborhood became "hood." In HHNL, rhyme was woven into phrases that have become part of mainstream culture. The hip-hop phrase

HIP-HOP NATION LANGUAGE DICTIONARY

The list below shows words from HHNL translated into Standard English. Many of these came into use in the 1990s.

- Bootsee: When a person is acting/dressing in a showy way
- Cat: A fraud
- Choppin it up: Making conversation
- Communicator: Cell phone
- Fedi: Money
- Mail: A check
- Marinatin: Thinking about a subject
- Pimpin: Being rich
- Sahob: Friend
- Smell Me?: Do you understand?

Fab 5 Freddy, former host of *Yo! MTV Raps,* collected rap slang into a book called *Fresh Fly Flavor: Words and Phrases of the Hip Hop Generation* in 1992.

"in it to win it" has been around since the 1990s.[2] Hillary Clinton used this exact slogan when she announced her candidacy for president in 2015. The language of hip-hop reflects speech patterns of different regions of the country. For example, rapper Master P has a characteristic phrase, "Ya heeeaaard may?" (you heard me?).[3] This is the distinctive sound of Southern hip-hop.

N.W.A's lead rapper, Ice Cube, was known for his controversial and explicit lyrics.

An attitude of rebellion and resistance peeks out of HHNL vocabulary. A word that describes a problem is flipped to mean the opposite. For example, to convey that something is *good*, a HHNL speaker will say the thing is *bad*. When a person is *down* in HHNL, he is *up* for doing something. The word *nigger* has a long and ugly past in US history. Members of the hip-hop generation realized the word had one meaning inside their culture and another meaning outside it. So they changed the spelling. An "er" on the end of the word remains a racial slur. But within hip-hop culture, when "er" is replaced with "a," the word means a good friend. Proponents say that by redefining the word, HHNL has removed the negative power the N-word has had for hundreds of years. That said, it's still not accepted for non–African Americans and those outside of hip-hop culture to use the word *nigga*.

Hip-hop artists have played a key role in expanding the vocabulary of HHNL. The rapper E-40 has created some of the most unique slang phrases, from flamboastin

> "The things I say come from the life that I used to live. . . . Most of you all don't know what it's like to have to sell some dope or you aren't going to have nothing to eat for the next three days. Most of you all don't know what that life is like."[4]
>
> —Rapper T.I. on censorship

(flamboyant and boasting) to po-po (police). Graffiti writers were the first to coin the term *phat*, which means excellent. The choice of "ph" to replace "f" is an example of how hip-hop language strives for unique expressions that set speakers apart from the mainstream.

Censorship

As gangsta rap and other hip-hop subgenres became more mainstream, its lyrics increasingly upset moral watchdogs. The group N.W.A faced trouble putting on tours because of the song "F*** Tha Police." Police officers who moonlighted as security guards refused to work the group's concerts, and shows had to be canceled. When the group played the song at a Detroit, Michigan, concert, police stormed the stage, ending the show. A US district court ruled that 2 Live Crew's 1989 album, *As Nasty as They Wanna Be*, was obscene and banned its sale. Members of the group were arrested after a performance

WARNING—EXPLICIT LYRICS

The Parents Music Resource Center was formed in the 1980s over concern about rock music that referenced violence, drugs, and the devil. The organization urged the music industry to adopt a rating system and label all albums. Rock musician Frank Zappa was outraged. In response, he created his own label. By the early 1990s, hip-hop albums had become the target for censorship, but sales of rap music remained high.

PARENTAL ADVISORY EXPLICIT LYRICS

In the 1990s, bold black-and-white parental advisory stickers began appearing on albums that included explicit lyrics.

and charged with obscenity, although the verdict was later overturned.

Politicians fanned public concerns about HHNL. In 1991, US Representative Newt Gingrich encouraged businesses to pull advertising from radio stations that played hip-hop music. Labels that cautioned buyers about explicit lyrics were a fixture on CD covers by the mid-1990s. To please big chain stores, the music industry bleeped offensive lyrics and airbrushed cover art. Artists had to choose to either sing what was in their hearts or sing what they could sell.

An International Language

Hip-hop language is having radical effects on nations far from the shores of the United States. In the winter of 2010, the young Tunisian rapper El Général put his song "Mr. President" on YouTube. The lyrics condemned the Tunisian leader Zine al-Abidine Ben Ali's oppressive rule. El Général was imprisoned, fueling protests by his fans that contributed to Ben Ali's overthrow.

Tunisia is not the only nation where the language of hip-hop is striking at the power structure. Kleber Gomes grew up in the favelas, or slums, of São Paulo, Brazil. Under the name Criolo, which means a mixed-race person, he raps about the racism that confronts the descendants of enslaved people in Brazil, and he calls for economic justice.

COVERED UP

Hip-hop culture has been censored for visual art as well as lyrics. Warner Bros. dropped Ice-T when he refused to alter the cover art for his 1992 album *Home Invasion*. The cover depicted a white child listening to music. Next to the boy was a stack of tapes by other rappers, including Ice Cube and Public Enemy. Fantasies swirl around the boy's head. Men in ski masks beat up a white man. Another man tears the clothes off a black woman. Ice-T released the record with Priority Records in 1993.

HHNL has also revived and transformed existing languages. There were no rhymes in Japanese until rappers introduced them into the language. British colonization of Hong Kong made English the language of power and culture, even though 90 percent of the people of the territory were native Cantonese speakers.[5] After hip-hop musicians began to rap in Cantonese, the language became respected and used again.

The Hip-Hop Nation has no borders. The only passport needed to enter is an understanding and appreciation of hip-hop culture. This language of words, gestures, and beats links poor and disenfranchised people from different societies as they try to tell the world who they are.

ENDANGERED LANGUAGES

When European powers colonized many parts of the world, they suppressed native languages. Cultures with no written language began to slide toward extinction as native speakers died and traditions and history were forgotten. Today hip-hop is emerging as a tool to preserve cultural history and motivate indigenous youth to keep their ancestral languages alive. The hip-hop group Nuuk Posse in Greenland raps in Danish, English, and Kalaallisut, the language of the Inuit people of the island. Wayna Rap is doing the same thing in Bolivia. The group raps in Aymara, a native Indian language, but puts Spanish subtitles on their videos so non-Aymara speakers can also understand their fiery lyrics.

8
STAGE AND
SCREEN

In 2016, the Broadway musical *Hamilton* won 11 Tony Awards, one short of a record.[1] What is unusual about the honors heaped on this performance is that *Hamilton* is a biography of US founding father Alexander Hamilton, and the play is steeped in hip-hop culture. The show's success demonstrates how hip-hop has made its presence felt on the stage and screen.

Comedy Television

The first glimpse of hip-hop culture on prime-time television was squeaky clean. Rapper Will Smith starred in *The Fresh Prince of Bel-Air* from 1990 to 1996. He played a boy from the inner city who was sent to live with wealthy

Theatergoers line up to see the acclaimed musical *Hamilton* in New York in November 2016.

Actor and rapper Will Smith appears on the set of his hit television show, *The Fresh Prince of Bel-Air*, in the 1990s.

relatives in a Los Angeles mansion. Themes were light, and Smith's rap lyrics were tame.

Russell Simmons, founder of Def Jam Recordings, teamed up with HBO to produce *Def Comedy Jam* and revealed a much more raw image of hip-hop culture. Thirty minutes of comedy unlike anything the United States had seen before came on television each Friday night in 1992. Mainly African-American stand-up comics were featured. The comedy was raunchy, and the themes explored were dark, including police brutality, racism, and AIDS.

At first *Def Comedy Jam* was praised because African-American comedians finally had an opportunity to take center stage. The show launched the careers of Dave Chappelle, Martin Lawrence, Chris Tucker, and more. But by 1994, opposition stiffened to the language used in the

YO! MTV RAPS

Two years before *The Fresh Prince of Bel-Air* premiered, Will Smith was one of the artists who introduced the first episode of *Yo! MTV Raps*. For one hour, *Yo! MTV Raps* focused entirely on hip-hop music, giving airtime to artists who were rarely played on the network. The show, which ran from 1988 through 1995, was extremely popular with young black viewers. It also introduced mainstream audiences in the United States to hip-hop music and culture. Many of the stars who first appeared on *Yo! MTV Raps* went on to star in Hollywood movies and television shows.

Russell Simmons, founder of Def Jam Recordings and Def Comedy Jam, is pictured in the showroom for his clothing label, Phat Farm.

program. For example, in a five-minute stand-up routine, comedian Joe Torry used 63 vulgar words, or one almost every five seconds.[2]

African-American critics said the show heightened racial stereotypes. They felt the culture on *Def Comedy Jam* did not represent them, and they resented the sentiment that hip-hop culture was the only authentically black culture. Still, the program ran through 1997 and again in 2006.

From 2000 through 2001, *The Lyricist Lounge Show* aired on MTV. Filmed live, the show featured comedy sketches, rap, and hip-hop music. The concept for the show came from a New York City club of the same name founded by Danny Castro and Anthony Marshall. The club helped launch the careers of hip-hop artists Sean Combs, Eminem, and the Notorious B.I.G.

Hip-Hop in Film

The image of hip-hop culture on the big screen has evolved over the past 40 years. In the 1980s, the few hip-hop movies made were semibiographical. The first and most influential of these was *Wild Style* in 1983. The two main characters, graffiti artists Zoro and Rose, were played by two real-life graffiti writers, Lee and Lady Pink. Almost every character in the movie was played by real hip-hop artists. *Wild Style* was important because it showed

REALITY WITH LAUGHS

Russell Simmons believed his show *Def Comedy Jam* communicated aspects of hip-hop culture the American public could not hear anywhere else. He realized the obscenities offended some people, but he encouraged them to listen closely to the messages underneath the vulgarity. Simmons said, "If [the comedians] are not as positive as you would like them to be, you have to listen to them and understand them. It's a dose of reality."[3]

the culture to people outside of the neighborhoods where it originated.

Following *Wild Style*, similar low-budget movies were made. Their story lines were weak, but these films highlighted the music, lyrics, dance, and art of hip-hop culture. *Beat Street*, *Breakin'*, and *Breakin' 2: Electric Boogaloo* all featured performances loosely based on the real lives of the artists who appeared in the films.

WOMEN'S ROLES

Two 1990s hip-hop films stand out for giving women roles outside the love interest or mother. *New Jack City*, released in 1991, starred Vanessa Williams as the chief of security for a high-ranking company executive. She is a woman with power as she advises her boss and commits murder as part of her job. In 1996, *Set It Off* featured four black female bank robbers who turned to crime out of desperation. They approach the job with business sense, confidence, and strength. Although hip-hop culture has been criticized for either ignoring or demeaning women, these two examples show women in positions of power.

Life in the hood was the theme of 1990s movies. During this decade, drug use and gang warfare put urban areas in the news, and gangsta rap was popular. In 1991, *Boyz n the Hood* hit theaters. The movie about three black boys growing up in South Central Los Angeles starred rapper Ice Cube, a founding member of N.W.A.

Boyz n the Hood was the first coming-of-age film for the hip-hop generation.

In this scene from the groundbreaking movie *Boyz n the Hood*, Ice Cube plays Doughboy, who is out to avenge his half brother's death.

With grim reality, it portrayed blacks under siege from drugs, violence, and crime. Underpinning the film was the struggle to find meaning in life. When the character Doughboy loses his brother to street violence and his mother is alienated from him, Doughboy accepts that everyone has abandoned him. When he says, "Either they don't know, don't show, or don't care about what's going on in the hood," Doughboy is referring to a society that has forgotten urban black America.[4]

Boyz n the Hood was a box office smash and garnered two Academy Award nominations. Its success spawned a series of other films that tried but failed to create a realistic portrayal of the hip-hop generation. Black youth were characterized as thugs, and the films fostered a national, even global, backlash against young black men.

In the 2000s, films have tended to feature hip-hop stars rather than focus heavily on the culture. From Queen Latifah to Ja Rule to Bow Wow, rappers have starred in action movies, romantic comedies, and everything in between. Film executives finally realized that hip-hop sells. If a famous rapper is cast in a film, fans will pay to see the movie.

> "Black gangster films have helped to shape a generation's consciousness.... Where they are wrong, the misinformation... contributes to the crisis in African American culture."[5]
>
> —*Bakari Kitwana in* The Hip Hop Generation: Young Blacks and the Crisis in African-American Culture

Hip-Hop on Stage

Putting on a Broadway show requires a lot of money, and hip-hop stars have invested in award-winning shows featuring black artists. In 2009, rapper Jay Z and rapper-turned-actor Will Smith helped produce the play *Fela!*, a musical about the life of Nigerian composer and activist Fela Anikulapo Kuti. In 2004, Combs invested and starred in the reproduction of the classic *A Raisin in the Sun*. The audience for this play was 80 percent black, and high ticket sales proved black audiences would attend theatrical productions, especially when a hip-hop icon was on stage.[6]

Most recently, Lin-Manuel Miranda wrote the musical *Hamilton,* bringing hip-hop to Broadway once more. The play opened in the fall of 2015 to critical acclaim and box office success and has become a cultural phenomenon.

SHAKESPEAREAN RAP

The Q Brothers, Gregory and Jeffrey Qaiyum, are two Chicago siblings who translate Shakespeare's plays into hip-hop performances. In the Q Brothers' hands, Shakespeare's *Othello* became *Othello: The Remix, Much Ado About Nothing* became *Funk It Up about Nothin',* and *The Comedy of Errors* was transformed into *The Bomb-itty of Errors*. On the schedule for 2017 was *Romeo and Juliet*. The brothers intended to cast a pair of Chicago teens to play the ill-fated lovers, seeking youth "with rap in their blood and bones."[7]

Miranda put hip-hop twists on the tale. The historical leaders of the American Revolution (1775–1783) were all white, but *Hamilton's* cast is multiracial. Leslie Odom Jr., who played Vice President Aaron Burr until leaving the show in July 2016, said, "It is quite literally taking the

Hamilton took pop and hip-hop culture by storm as Tracee Ellis Ross and Anthony Anderson performed a skit from the show at the BET Awards show in June 2016.

history that someone has tried to exclude us from and reclaiming it."[8]

The show is almost entirely in song. Debates among President Washington's cabinet members are performed as rap battles, and references to hip-hop culture are peppered throughout the play. Celebrities from Jay Z, Eminem, and Nas to Barack Obama, Bernie Sanders, and Hillary Clinton have sat transfixed as the musical took them on a historical journey.

Miranda realized most people could not afford tickets, so he started an educational initiative. This program brings in tens of thousands of low-income children annually to see the play. The magic of the screen and stage has the power to communicate hip-hop culture to the next generation and helps the elites meet the culture of the streets.

BEHIND HAMILTON

Alexander Hamilton spent his youth as a poor orphan on the Caribbean island of Nevis but rose to become an aide to General George Washington and later the first treasury secretary of the United States. As a teenager, Hamilton wrote an essay about how bad the environment was in which he was living, which helped him escape the island. Lin-Manuel Miranda, the author of *Hamilton*, recognized a similarity in how men like Jay Z or Eminem each wrote their way out of obscurity. Rap was the natural way to tell Hamilton's rags-to-riches story.

9 HIP-HOP ACTIVISM

More than 50 years after the civil rights movement pushed the United States down a path toward greater racial equality, many obstacles still confront African Americans. Forty-two percent of black children attend school in high-poverty neighborhoods. African Americans make up 13.2 percent of the general population, but they comprise 37 percent of the nation's homeless. Blacks are jailed nearly six times more often than whites.[1] Today, activists in the hip-hop community are working to create a more equitable society.

Rapper Sean Combs, *front*, and singer Mary J. Blige, *right*, lead a Promote
the Vote rally for Barack Obama in 2008.

History of Socially Conscious Rap

Hip-hop culture has been a voice for the urban poor since it began. Grandmaster Flash and the Furious Five released "The Message" in 1982. With alternating anger and despair, the group rapped about living among roaches, the smell of urine, and people waiting in the alley with baseball bats.

Between 1988 and 1994, rappers joined forces to produce posse cuts, musical collaborations for a common cause. After a fatal fight during a 1988 concert, rapper KRS-One teamed up with 13 other artists to record "Self Destruction." All proceeds from the song were donated to the National Urban League. A year later, when the crack cocaine drug epidemic was raging, the West Coast Rap All-Stars recorded "We're All in the Same Gang." Through these unified efforts, rappers raised money for and increased awareness of issues that faced urban communities.

As corporate America invested in hip-hop culture in the 1990s, however, celebrity entertainers and athletes fell silent. Individual community organizers continued to work for change, but there was no large social movement spearheaded by figures young hip-hoppers would follow.

Hip-hop artist KRS-One spoke out against violence at the VH-1 Hip Hop Honors event in October 2008.

Celebrities feared losing corporate contracts if they took a controversial stand.

A Wake-Up Call

In August 2005, Hurricane Katrina devastated New Orleans, Louisiana, a city that was mostly black and poor. The local and national government's response to the storm was slow and inadequate, and the death toll from the storm was likely more than 1,800.[2] Many people in the hip-hop community believed the reason the administration of President George W. Bush was slow to respond to the crisis was because many of the victims were black.

The music created after Hurricane Katrina revealed how blacks of New Orleans were suffering from a dual tragedy—the destructive hurricane and governmental neglect. In the song "Katrina Clap," rapper Mos Def begins with the story of a lady who survived the flood and was discovered days later by rescue workers. The rescuers ask how she survived and where she had been. The woman

Mos Def has a history of advocacy. In this video he speaks out against police brutality.

responded, "Where you been?" In the song's final line, Mos Def says, "Don't talk about it, be about it."[3] One year after the storm, Mos Def performed the song on the back of a flatbed truck outside the MTV Video Music Awards. He was immediately arrested for disorderly conduct and for not having a permit to perform.

Hip-Hop and Politics

Most politicians avoid hip-hop because of the controversy the genre spawns, but Barack Obama embraced it when he ran for president in 2008. During the campaign, he was interviewed on Black Entertainment Television and asked if he liked hip-hop. Obama replied, "Of course."[4]

By the summer of 2008, Obama had won the Democratic nomination, and rappers including Lil Wayne, Nas, Jay Z, and Ludacris performed songs about him. Other artists admitted they would be voting for the first time in their lives—for Obama. Fans of these celebrities also became fans of Obama, and on Election Day they turned out in record numbers. The voting rate among college-age students was the highest it had been in 35 years, and for the first time in the nation's history, young blacks voted in higher numbers than whites.[5] Barack Obama was elected, becoming the first black president.

COMMUNITY ORGANIZING

For decades, members of the hip-hop generation have been involved in small-scale social movements in communities across the country. Youth Speaks is an organization in San Francisco, California, that works to get spoken-word poetry in educational institutions across the Bay Area. The Central Brooklyn Cop Watch monitors the use of force by police. Other activist organizations lead AIDS awareness campaigns in black communities, work to abolish the death penalty, and fight to reduce the incarceration rates of young black women.

However, the love affair between Obama and the hip-hop community did not last. Activists felt let down that Obama did not work harder to address problems in the black community. Disillusioned about the power of the federal government to make meaningful change, some activists began taking action into their own hands.

Black Lives Matter

A series of high-profile police killings of unarmed African-American men in the mid-2010s caused grief and outrage in black communities, leading to a mass movement called Black Lives Matter.

In February 2012, 17-year-old Trayvon Martin, a black teen who was carrying no weapons, was shot by George Zimmerman, a neighborhood watch volunteer. After a lengthy trial, Zimmerman was acquitted. The verdict stunned and demoralized African Americans, but it also spurred three young women to take action. Opal Tometi, Patrisse Cullors, and Alicia Garza created social media accounts with the hashtag #blacklivesmatter and encouraged people to share their stories. Then another death set a fire under the fledgling movement.

On August 9, 2014, 18-year-old Michael Brown, also unarmed, was killed by a white police officer in Ferguson, Missouri. Protests rocked the city, and people held signs and shouted the slogan "Black Lives Matter." The rallying cry grew louder as several more unarmed black men were shot by police over subsequent months.

Black Lives Matter is different from the organized civil rights movement of the 1950s and 1960s. There is no Martin Luther King Jr. to represent the face of the campaign. Black Lives Matter is a collection of different actions led by

REALIST OR CYNIC

In 2004, Combs launched the "Vote or Die" campaign to register young people to vote. However, by the 2016 presidential election, Combs seemed to have become a skeptic. When asked about how to encourage youth to vote, Combs dismissed voting as a "scam." He said the black community has become disenfranchised because they do not see results from politicians. "At the end of the day I'm not telling you not to vote," Combs said. "But I'm saying be a realist . . ."[6]

At this Black Lives Matter rally in Washington, DC, on December 13, 2014, protesters demanded an end to police brutality.

young community leaders across the country who do not always work together. But they are united by a concern about the injustices facing blacks, and they are linked by social media.

Hip-hop's celebrities, like their fans, are also taking a stand. After more police shootings in the summer of 2016, at least a dozen hip-hop and R&B artists recorded songs focusing on the use of force by police.

The song "Alright" by Kendrick Lamar became a sort of anthem for the Black Lives Matter movement. In July 2016, activists were boarding buses after a conference at Cleveland State University. When they spotted police arresting a 14-year-old boy on suspicion of bringing alcohol on the bus, the activists began to question the police.

Kendrick Lamar is credited with uniting the Black Lives Matter movement under a common song, "Alright."

The situation quickly escalated. The police used pepper spray on the activists, and this drew more people to the scene. Approximately 200 people had gathered, and the situation was ripe for violence. After the boy was released to his mother, someone started to chant, "We gon be alright. We gon be alright"—the chorus line from the song.[7] Eventually, the crowd dispersed. The song represents a powerful statement that despite serious challenges, the people of hip-hop will endure.

The Future

Hip-hop is a living and evolving culture. In 1973, it was limited to the South Bronx, where DJs played records on dual turntables, MCs fought duels with words, and b-boys and b-girls battled in cyphers before walls that were graffiti masterpieces. The culture went through its adolescence of gangsta rap and corporate control, of censorship and culture wars. Today hip-hop culture is being redefined on a global stage.

> "Hip-hop has always been about having fun, but it's also about taking responsibility. And now we have a platform to speak our minds. Millions of people are watching us. Let's hear something powerful."[8]
>
> —DJ Kool Herc

For children of the ghetto, rap music still represents a ticket out of poverty. But in contemporary hip-hop culture, two schools of thought have emerged. Some argue that hip-hop has never been more commercialized. Its worldwide popularity gives rappers even greater opportunities to market their music and message on a global scale. Others in the hip-hop community are actively resisting the commercialization of the art form. This culture began as a vehicle for the voiceless to speak out against the economic and political institutions that oppressed them. Today hip-hop is once again serving as a microphone for those who feel invisible and forgotten. The question is—will the world listen?

BEHIND
THE SONG

"DON'T SHOOT"

When Michael Brown was shot to death by a Ferguson, Missouri, police officer on August 9, 2014, rapper The Game felt he had to speak up. So he coordinated with other well-known rappers to produce the single "Don't Shoot." It is a song of tribute and protest.

Each artist takes the lead on a different verse, and the lyrics reveal shared outrage and a call for action, although ideas about what that action should be vary. The Game raps concern about the rage that followed Brown's death. "Mothers crying stop the riots, we ain't got to chalk the city." He is cautioning listeners against violent protests that could result in more deaths.

A line from Rick Ross's verse seems to contradict The Game's restraint. He raps, "Now we throwing Molotovs in this holocaust." Whether Ross is encouraging protesters to throw firebombs or just describing events in Ferguson is unclear.

The chorus declares it is "Time to take a stand and save our future." In unison the singers declare they are putting up their hands so they do not get shot. These words are particularly poignant in the last chorus when The Game's young daughter sings solo. Her high-pitched voice haunts the listener as she sings the final line: "Don't point your weapons at me."[9]

One of The Game's musical inspirations is N.W.A.

TIMELINE

1972

CHARMIN 65 tags the Statue of Liberty.

1973

In August, Clive "Kool Herc" Campbell deejays his first party in the South Bronx.

1975

Early pieces of hip-hop culture take shape as Afrika Bambaataa forms the Universal Zulu Nation, DJ Grandmaster Flash begins to mix music, and teenage DJ Theodore Livingston invents scratching.

1979

Sylvia Robinson organizes the Sugarhill Gang, and together they record the first commercial hip-hop song, "Rapper's Delight."

1982

Battle rap begins with the first standoff between Kool Moe Dee and Busy Bee Starski.

1983

The movie *Wild Style* is released, the first Hollywood film featuring hip-hop culture.

1988

N.W.A releases the album *Straight Outta Compton*, raising controversy about gangsta rap; *Yo! MTV Raps* first airs on MTV.

1992

The clothing design company FUBU is founded; *Def Comedy Jam* premiers on HBO.

1996

In September, Tupac Shakur is shot and killed.

1997

In March, the Notorious B.I.G. is shot and killed.

2004

The Ladies of Hip-Hop Festival is founded.

2005

In August, Hurricane Katrina devastates New Orleans, Louisiana, and the government's slow response angers members of the hip-hop community.

2008

Barack Obama wins the presidential election with some help from the hip-hop community.

2012

Activists create the hashtag #blacklivesmatter, which develops into a grassroots civil rights movement aimed at combating excessive force by police against African Americans.

2016

The hip-hop musical *Hamilton* wins 11 Tony Awards.

ESSENTIAL
FACTS

KEY PLAYERS

- DJ Kool Herc was the first to figure out how to play extended breaks on records.

- DJ Grandmaster Flash was the first to mix records using two turntables and a mixer.

- Doug E. Fresh, known as the first human beatbox, is credited with introducing the hip-hop community to beatboxing.

- Afrika Bambaataa founded the Universal Zulu Nation in 1975, and decided to use music to improve his community. He brought DJs, dancers, graffiti writers, and MCs together at the Bronx River Community Center.

TRENDS

- The founding elements of hip-hop culture were established in the 1970s by Afrika Bambaataa and the Zulu Nation.

- The mid-1970s through the mid-1980s were when graffiti writing and B-boying had the strongest hold in popular culture. By the end of the 1980s, b-boying was left behind as rappers took up recording careers, and graffiti declined because cities cracked down on the practice.

- The mid-1980s are generally considered the golden age of hip-hop music because of the variety of sounds and quality of lyrics; this is also when hip-hop began spreading internationally.

- The late 1980s through the late 1990s was the era of gangsta rap. The music reflected the gritty side of urban street life.

- In the early 2000s, the sale of rap music declined, and the popularity of gangsta rap faded.

- Hip-hop youth became more politically involved in both the election of the first black president and in grassroots movements combating the excessive use of force by law enforcement.

LEGACY

Hip-hop culture informed the world about the realities of urban life for poor, black youth, a population that had been largely invisible before music, dance, and fashion shined a spotlight on it.

QUOTE

"Hip-hop has always been about having fun, but it's also about taking responsibility. And now we have a platform to speak our minds. Millions of people are watching us. Let's hear something powerful."

—*DJ Kool Herc*

GLOSSARY

BREAK
The instrumental section of a song, usually identified with a percussion solo.

CENSORSHIP
The act of imposing values on others by limiting what they may read, write, hear, or see.

CYPHER
The circle in which b-boys and b-girls performed.

FUNK MUSIC
Type of urban dance music African Americans began creating in the 1960s; it is a combination of jazz, soul, and rhythm and blues with a good dancing beat.

GANGSTA RAP
A type of rap music with lyrics featuring the violence and drug use of urban gang life.

GOLD
A certification for an album that has sold more than 500,000 copies.

HOMOPHOBIA
Fear of and hostility toward gay people.

INTELLECTUAL PROPERTY
An idea, invention, or process that came from someone's mind.

LINGUIST

A person who studies the structure of languages.

MIXER

An audio machine used by DJs to make smooth transitions between recorded sounds as they are being played.

MIXTAPE

A compilation of unreleased tracks, freestyle rap music, and DJ mixes of songs.

PRODUCER

The person who supervises the sampling, mixing, and recording of music and also guides the performers.

RACISM

Inferior treatment of a person or group of people based on race.

TAG

A graffiti writer's signature, the most basic form of graffiti, or the act of signing one's tag.

TURNTABLE

An electronic device consisting of a needle and a disk that spins. When the needle is placed on a vinyl record, it plays music.

VINYL RECORD

A disc made of vinyl plastic on which music has been recorded.

ADDITIONAL
RESOURCES

SELECTED BIBLIOGRAPHY

Bynoe, Yvonne. *Encyclopedia of Rap and Hip-hop Culture.*
Westport, CT: Greenwood, 2006. Print.

Chang, Jeff. *Can't Stop Won't Stop: A History of the Hip-Hop Generation.* New York: St. Martin's, 2005. Print.

Coates, Ta-Nehisi. *Between the World and Me.* New York: Spiegel & Grau, 2015. Print.

Kitwana, Bakari. *The Hip-Hop Generation: Young Blacks and the Crisis in African-American Culture.* New York: BasicCivitas, 2002. Print.

FURTHER READINGS

Baker, Soren. *The History of Rap and Hip-Hop.* Detroit, MI: Lucent, 2012. Print.

Edwards, Paul. *How to Rap: The Art and Science of the Hip-Hop MC.* Chicago: Chicago Review, 2009. Print.

Piskor, Ed. *Hip-Hop Family Tree.* Seattle: Fantagraphics, 2013. Print.

WEBSITES

To learn more about Hip-Hop Insider, visit **abdobooklinks.com**. These links are routinely monitored and updated to provide the most current information available.

FOR MORE INFORMATION

For more information on this subject, contact or visit the following organizations:

NATIONAL MUSEUM OF AFRICAN AMERICAN HISTORY AND CULTURE
1400 Constitution Avenue NW
Washington, DC, 20560
1-844-750-3012
https://nmaahc.si.edu/
This Smithsonian museum has an exhibit titled *Musical Crossroads*. It traces the evolution of African-American music from the time Africans first arrived in colonial North America up to the present, including the evolution of hip-hop.

ROCK STEADY PARK
West 98th Street and Amsterdam Avenue
New York, New York, 10025
New York City Parks Department
https://www.nycgovparks.org/parks/
happy-warrior-playground/history
This park is where the Rock Steady Crew once hung out. At one time the group numbered more than 500 members. This park is also called the Happy Warrior Playground.

CHAPTER 1. BORN FROM ASHES

1. Jeff Chang. *Can't Stop Won't Stop: A History of the Hip-Hop Generation*. New York: St. Martin's, 2005. Print. 69.

2. Emmett G. Price III. *Hip-Hop Culture*. Santa Barbara, CA: ABC CLIO, 2006. Print. 5–7.

3. Jeff Chang. *Can't Stop Won't Stop: A History of the Hip-Hop Generation*. New York: St. Martin's, 2005. Print. xi.

4. Emmett G. Price III. *Hip-Hop Culture*. Santa Barbara, CA: ABC CLIO, 2006. Print. 5.

5. Jeff Chang. *Can't Stop Won't Stop: A History of the Hip-Hop Generation*. New York: St. Martin's, 2005. Print. 15–17.

6. Ibid. 12–13.

7. Emmett G. Price III. *Hip-Hop Culture*. Santa Barbara, CA: ABC CLIO, 2006. Print. 5.

8. Bill Dotson. "Expanding the Definition of Hip-hop Culture." *USC News*. University of Southern California, 15 Oct. 2007. Web. 12 Oct. 2016.

9. Owen Moritz. "Looters Prey on the City during the Blackout of 1977." *New York Daily News*. New York Daily News, 15 July 1977. Web. 2 Oct. 2016.

CHAPTER 2. FROM DJ TO PRODUCER

1. Angus Batey. "DJ Kool Herc DJs His First Block Party (His Sister's Birthday) at 1520 Sedgwick Avenue, Bronx, New York." *Guardian*. Guardian News and Media, 12 June 2011. Web. 2 Oct. 2016.

2. "Mercedes Ladies." *Old School Hip-Hop*. Old School Hip Hop, 7 Jan. 2010. Web. 31 Oct. 2016.

CHAPTER 3. RAPPING MCs

1. Jeff Chang. *Can't Stop Won't Stop: A History of the Hip-Hop Generation*. New York: St. Martin's, 2005. Print. 113.

2. Ibid.

3. Ibid. 82.

4. KRS-One. "Hip-Hop vs. Rap." *Genius.com*. Genius Media Group, n.d. Web. 27 Oct. 2016.

5. "N.W.A Bio." *Rolling Stone*. Rolling Stone, n.d. Web. 19 Oct. 2016.

6. Jeff Chang. *Can't Stop Won't Stop: A History of the Hip-Hop Generation*. New York: St. Martin's, 2005. Print. 314–315.

7. Tim Shipman. "Gangsta Rap on Death Row as the US Tunes Out." *Telegraph*. Telegraph Media Group, 1 July 2007. Web. 20 Oct. 2016.

8. Michael Eric Dyson. "Tupac: Life Goes On. Why The Rapper Still Appeals to Fans and Captivates Scholars a Decade after His Death." *Black Issues Book Review* 8.5 (2006): 14–18. *Academic Search Premier*. Web. 7 Oct. 2016.

CHAPTER 4. TAGGING AND BOMBING

1. Jeff Chang. *Can't Stop Won't Stop: A History of the Hip-Hop Generation*. New York: St. Martin's, 2005. Print. 73.

2. Randy Kennedy. "Celebrating Forefathers of Graffiti." *New York Times*. New York Times, 22 July 2011. Web. 16 Oct. 2016.

3. "Graffiti in Its Own Words." *New York Magazine*. New York Media, 2011. Web. 16 Oct. 2016.

4. Ibid.

5. Roger Gastman and Caleb Neelon. *The History of American Graffiti*. New York: Harper, 2010. Print. 23.

6. Jeff Chang. *Can't Stop Won't Stop: A History of the Hip-Hop Generation*. New York: St. Martin's, 2005. Print. 124.

7. Roger Gastman and Caleb Neelon. *The History of American Graffiti*. New York: Harper, 2010. Print. 28.

8. Ibid.

9. Ibid.

10. Ibid. 230.

11. Leslie W. Rabine. "These Walls Belong to Everybody: The Graffiti Art Movement in Dakar." *African Studies Quarterly* 14.3 (2014): 89–112. *Academic Search Premier*. Web. 20 Oct. 2016.

CHAPTER 5. ROCKING AND POPPING

1. Jeff Chang. *Can't Stop Won't Stop: A History of the Hip-Hop Generation*. New York: St. Martin's, 2005. Print. 80.

2. Ibid. 75.

3. Ibid. 115.

4. "How *Soul Train* Got America Dancing." *Talk of the Nation*. NPR, 9 Feb. 2010. Web. 16 Feb. 2017.

5. Jeff Chang. *Can't Stop Won't Stop: A History of the Hip-Hop Generation*. New York: St. Martin's Press, 2005. Print. 118.

6. Ibid. 117.

7. Siobhan Burke. "Not Such a Man's World." *Dance Magazine* 86.11 (2012): 48–52. *Academic Search Premier*. Web. 20 Oct. 2016.

8. Heather Wisner. "From Street to Studio: Hip-Hop Comes Inside." *Dance Magazine* 80.9 (2006): 74–76. *Academic Search Premier*. Web. 16 Feb. 2017.

CHAPTER 6. LOOKING FRESH

1. Lauren Cochrane. "So Fresh and So Clean: A Brief History of Fashion and Hip-Hop." *Guardian*. Guardian News and Media, 27 Oct. 2015. Web. 20 Oct. 2016.

2. Ibid.

3. Stephanie Smith-Strickland. "How Rappers Took Over the World of Fashion." Highsnobiety. Tital Media, 15 Jan. 2016. Web. 23 Oct. 2016.

4. Ibid.

5. Jancee Dunn. "How Hip-Hop Style Bum-Rushed The Mall." *Rolling Stone* 808 (1999): 54. *Academic Search Premier.* Web. 20 Oct. 2016.

6. Karizza Sanchez. "Top Gear: The Oral History of Hip-Hop's Love Affair with Tommy Hilfiger." *Complex Style.* Complex, 22 Aug. 2016. Web. 23 Oct. 2016.

7. Ibid.

8. Ibid.

9. Jancee Dunn. "How Hip-Hop Style Bum-Rushed The Mall." *Rolling Stone* 808 (1999): 54. *Academic Search Premier.* Web. 20 Oct. 2016.

10. Arcynta Ali Childs. "From Brooklyn, a Rap Campaign against Tight Clothes." *Village Voice.* Village Voice, 24 June 2008. Web. 16 Feb. 2017.

11. Stephanie Smith-Strickland. "How Rappers Took Over the World of Fashion." *Highsnobiety.* Tital Media, 15 Jan. 2016. Web. 23 Oct. 2016.

CHAPTER 7. SPEAKING HIP-HOP

1. "Hip-Hop Nation." *Do You Speak American?* PBS, n.d. Web. 20 Oct. 2016.

2. William Safire. "On Language; The Rap on Hip-Hop." *New York Times.* New York Times, 8 Nov. 1992. Web. 24 Oct. 2016.

3. "Hip-Hop Nation." *Do You Speak American?* PBS, n.d. Web. 20 Oct. 2016.

4. Gail Mitchell. "50 Cent, T.I. Speak Their Minds on Lyric Censorship." *Billboard.* Billboard, 17 May 2007. Web. 31 Oct. 2016.

5. Awad Ibrahim. "Race, Language and Globalization: What Can 'Global Hip-Hop Nation' Teach Us about Citizenship?" *YouTube.* YouTube, 13 April 2013. Web. 24 Oct. 2016.

CHAPTER 8. STAGE AND SCREEN

1. "Tony Awards 2016: 'Hamilton' Wins 11 Awards but Doesn't Break Record." *CBS News.* CBS, 13 June 2016. Web. 30 Oct. 2016.

2. John J. O'Connor. "The Curse of Incessant Cursing." *New York Times.* New York Times, 31 July 1994. Web. 24 Oct. 2016.

3. Greg Braxton. "Laughz N the Hood: Television: A Showcase for Unknown Black Comics, Russell Simmons' *Def Comedy Jam* Begins Its Second Season Friday on HBO." *Los Angeles Times.* Los Angeles Times, 6 Aug. 1992. Web. 24 Oct. 2016.

4. Bakari Kitwana. *The Hip-Hop Generation: Young Blacks and the Crisis in African-American Culture.* New York: BasicCivitas, 2002. Print. 126.

5. Ibid. 139.

6. Carolyn M Brown. "Taking Center Stage." *Black Enterprise* 42.5 (2011): 14. *Academic Search Premier.* Web. 20 Oct. 2016.

7. Chloe Taft. "The Rap's the Thing." *American Scholar* 85.1 (2016): 16. *Academic Search Premier.* Web. 20 Oct. 2016.

8. Mark Binelli. "Hamilton Mania." *Rolling Stone* 1263 (2016): 36–43. *Academic Search Premier.* Web. 20 Oct. 2016.

CHAPTER 9. HIP-HOP ACTIVISM

1. Elizabeth Day. "#BlackLivesMatter: The Birth of a New Civil Rights Movement." *Guardian*. Guardian News and Media, 19 July 2015. Web. 26 Oct. 2016.

2. Lindsey Cook and Ethan Rosenberg. "No One Knows How Many People Died in Katrina." *US News and World Report*. US News and World Report, 28 Aug. 2015. Web. 16 Feb. 2017.

3. Mary Ruth Marotte and Glen Jellenek. T*en Years After Katrina: Critical Perspectives of the Storm's Effect on American Culture and Identity*. Lanham, Maryland: Lexington, 2015. Google Books. Web. 25 Oct. 2016.

4. Sandford K. Richmond. "Paint The White House Black!! A Critical Discourse Analysis Look at Hip-Hop's Social, Cultural, and Political Influence on the Presidency of Barack Obama." *Western Journal of Black Studies* 37.4 (2013): 249–257. *Academic Search Premier*. Web. 20 Sept. 2016.

5. Erik Nielson and Travis Gosa. "Obama and Hip-Hop: A Breakup Song." *Washington Post*. Washington Post, 25 Sept. 2015. Web. 25 Oct. 2016.

6. Brennan William. "Diddy Offers Honest Advice to 2016 Voters." *HuffPost Multi Cultural*. Huffington Post, 21 Oct. 2015. Web. 25 Oct. 2016.

7. Jamilah King. "The Improbable Story of How Kendrick Lamar's 'Alright' Became a Protest Anthem." *Mic Daily*. Mic Network, 11 Feb. 2016. Web. 26 Oct. 2016.

8. Jeff Chang. *Can't Stop Won't Stop: A History of the Hip-Hop Generation*. New York: St. Martin's, 2005. Print. xiii.

9. "Don't Shoot." *Genius.com*. Genius Media, n.d. Web. 1 Nov. 2016.

INDEX

Austin, Emilio "Buddha Stretch," Jr., 50–51

Bambaataa, Afrika, 18–19, 44
Basil, Toni, 47
Beastie Boys, 26
Black Lives Matter, 90–94
Blanco the Don, 60
Brathwaite, Kamau, 64
Brown, James, 10, 44
Brown, Michael, 91, 96
Busy Bee Starski, 25–26
Byrd-McPhee, Michele, 48

Campbell, Cindy, 4, 8
Campbell, Clive "Kool Herc," 4–8, 10, 14, 15, 18, 42
Campbell, Don, 46
Castro, Danny, 77
Ceisler, Billy, 57
censorship, 68–69, 95
Clinton, Antoinette "Butterscotch," 17
Coke La Rock, 24
Colón, Richard "Crazy Legs", 47, 50
Combs, Sean "Puff Daddy," 30, 59, 60, 77, 81, 91
Criolo, 70
Curtis, Coltrane, 57

dance, 42–51
Dash, Damon, 52
DJ Grandmaster Caz, 10
DJ Jazzy Jay, 44
DJ Kool Herc. See Campbell, Clive
DJ Spivey, 17
DJ techniques
    beat juggling, 16–17, 20
    beatboxing, 17
    merry-go-round, 7, 14, 15

mixtapes, 20
quick-mix theory, 15
sampling, 19, 21
scratching, 12, 15–16, 17
turntablism, 17–18
Dr. Dre, 30

Ecko, Marc, 58
Eminem, 77, 83

fashion, 52–61
Fresh, Doug E., 17
FUBU, 58–59
Furious Five, 86

Game, The, 96
gangsta rap, 28, 30, 31, 68, 78, 95
Général, El, 70
graffiti, 10, 12, 14, 18, 32–40
Grand Puba, 57–58
Grandmaster Flash, 15, 18, 22, 86

Hilfiger, Tommy, 57–58
Hip-Hop Nation Language (HHNL), 62–67, 69, 71

Ice Cube, 70, 78
Ice-T, 70

Jay Z, 59, 60, 80, 83, 89
Jenkins, Sacha, 52

"Katrina Clap," 88
Kidd Creole, 24
Kitwana, Bakari, 61
Knight, Suge, 29
Kool Moe Dee, 25–26
KRS-One, 86
Kuti, Fela Anikulapo, 80–81

Lady Pink, 36, 77
Lamar, Kendrick, 93
Lawrence, Martin, 75
Lil Wayne, 89
Livingston, Theodore "Grand
   Wizard," 15–16
LL Cool J, 26, 59
Ludacris, 89

Mack, Craig, 30
Marley Marl, 19
Marshall, Anthony, 77
Martin, Trayvon, 90
Master P, 66
McDaniels, Darryl "DMC," 54
Melle Mel, 24
Minaj, Nicki, 20
Miranda, Lin-Manuel, 81, 83
Mos Def, 88–89
movies, 49, 75, 77–80
   Beat Street, 17, 78
   Boyz n the Hood, 78–80
   Death Wish, 38
   Flashdance, 49–50
   Straight Outta Compton, 28–29
   Wild Style, 38, 49, 77–78

Nas, 31, 83, 89
Niggaz With Attitude (N.W.A), 28,
   68, 78
Notorious B.I.G., 30, 77
Nuuk Posse, 71

Obama, Barack, 83, 89
Odom, Leslie, Jr., 81

Public Enemy, 26, 70

Q Brothers, 81
Queen Latifah, 26, 80
Quiñones, Adolfo, 47

Robinson, Sylvia, 28
Ross, Rick, 96
Run-D.M.C., 26, 49, 54–55

Salt-N-Pepa, 26
Shakur, Tupac, 30
Sheri Sher, 18
Simmons, Russell, 75–77
Smith, Will, 72, 75, 80
Snoop Dogg, 30
Spoonie Gee, 17
Sugarhill Gang, 19, 28

television, 72–77
   Def Comedy Jam, 75–76
   Fresh Prince of Bel-Air, The, 72, 73
   Grind, The, 50
   Lyricist Lounge Show, The, 77
   Party Machine, The, 50
   Solid Gold, 50
   Soul Train, 49
   Yo! MTV Raps, 75
theater, 80–83
Thug Slaughter Force, 60
Torry, Joe, 76
Treacherous Three, 17, 25

Universal Zulu Nation, 18–19

Wayna Rap, 71
West, Kanye, 61
West Coast Rap All-Stars, 86
Wiggins, Robert Keith "Cowboy,"
   22–24
Williams, Pharrell, 61
Williams, Vanessa, 78

ABOUT THE AUTHOR

Judy Dodge Cummings is a writer and former history teacher from Wisconsin. She has written numerous nonfiction books for children and teenagers. Her other title about hip-hop music is *Macklemore & Ryan Lewis: Grammy-Winning Hip-Hop Duo*.